SCOTTISH MURDER STORIES

A COLLECTION OF SOLVED AND UNSOLVED MURDERS

Kathryn Buchanan

BRADWELL
BOOKS

Published by Bradwell Books

9 Orgreave Close Sheffield S13 9NP

Email: books@bradwellbooks.co.uk

British Library Cataloguing in Publication Data: a catalogue record for this book is available from the British Library.

1st Edition

ISBN: 9781910551530

Design by: Mark Titterton

Photograph Credits: Kathryn Buchanan
(The Author) and indicated separately

Print: Gomer Press, Llandysul, Ceredigion SA44 4JL

CONTENTS

Introduction

Murder is not an everyday occurrence in Scotland but over the years there have been many murders, solved and unsolved, that have caught the public's attention. The death penalty was execution by hanging until the abolition of capital punishment for murder in 1965, but unlike England it was not 'hang by the neck until dead', so there are cases like 'Half-hangit Maggie', who was found to be alive, banging on the lid of her coffin on the way to her burial, who did not have to be hanged again and lived to a ripe old age. In the Grassmarket in Edinburgh, the pub, Maggie Dickson's, is named after her. Nearby is the Last Drop Pub where the condemned were given their last drink before they dropped through the scaffold's trapdoor.

Maggie Dickson's Pub in the Grassmarket, Edinburgh – The Author

The Last Drop Pub in Edinburgh's Grassmarket, where public executions took place most days between 1660 and 1784. The last person hanged in the Grassmarket was robber, James Andrew. – The Author

There are some famous cases in this book, such as Burke and Hare, who murdered people and sold their corpses to Dr Robert Knox for dissection. Helen McDougal, Burke's common-law wife, received a not proven verdict in court. In old Scots law the verdicts were *culpable*, *convict* or *clense*, and it was Cromwell who introduced the 'guilty' and 'not guilty' verdicts. However, after the Reformation these were dropped and 'proven' and 'not proven' were used. In 1712, at the trial of Samuel

Hope, the jury demanded to return a 'not guilty' verdict, so Scotland's three-verdict system came into use. Both the 'not guilty' and the 'not proven' verdicts result in the acquittal of the accused, and until 2011 they could not be tried again for the same crime, but the law of double jeopardy has now changed so this is no longer the case.

Despite all the murders mentioned in this book, Scotland is actually a pretty safe place. In the past ten years, the annual number of homicides has fallenl from 137 to 61. The most common method of killing is with a sharp instrument and over half the accused were under the influence of drink or drugs or both. New scientific methods have aided police investigations with fingerprinting being used since the late nineteenth century, resulting in criminals choosing to wear gloves.

The World's End Pub on the corner of the Royal Mile – The Author

However, by the 1930s scientists had found a way of lifting fingerprints from material such as the inside of discarded gloves. The use of DNA profiling has been another breakthrough in investigating crimes and has led to cold cases being solved, such as the brutal murders in 1977 of Christine Eadie and Helen Scott, who were beaten, assaulted and throttled with their own underwear, and their bodies dumped in East Lothian. They were last seen by their friends in the World's End pub in Edinburgh. In 2014, at the age of 69, their murderer was finally sentenced to 37 years' imprisonment and became the first person in Scotland to be retried after an acquittal following the changes to the double-jeopardy law.

Kathryn Buchanan

Murder, murder, polis,
Three stairs up,
The wummin oan the middle stair,
Hit me wi' a cup.

Ma heid's aw broken,
Ma eye's aw cut,
Murder, murder, polis,
Three stairs up!

(Traditional children's rhyme)

Burke and Hare

Up the close, an' doon the stair,

But an' ben wae Burke an' Hare.

Burke's the butcher; Hare's the thief,

Knox the boy that buys the beef!

(Traditional skipping rhyme)

BY THE LATE EIGHTEENTH CENTURY, EDINBURGH WAS WELL ESTABLISHED AS A CITY WITH A STRONG REPUTATION FOR MEDICAL EXCELLENCE. THE UNIVERSITY WAS EXPANDING, WITH GROWING DEMAND FOR PLACES ON MEDICAL DEGREE COURSES, AND ROBERT KNOX (1791–1862), A FORMER ARMY SURGEON, ESTABLISHED AN ANATOMICAL SCHOOL. BY 1826 HIS LECTURES, WHICH APPEALED TO GENTLEMEN AS WELL AS MEDICAL STUDENTS, WERE ATTRACTING AUDIENCES OF UP TO 500 PEOPLE.

To enable students and doctors to continue with their anatomical studies into the working of the human body, a continuous supply of cadavers was required. By the early 1800s, demand was outstripping supply, and although doctors were allowed to use the bodies of executed criminals and those who died in prison, the allocation to Edinburgh Medical College was only five corpses per year. This poor supply of bodies for dissection brought out the entrepreneurial skill of the 'resurrectionists', who robbed new graves knowing they could sell a fresh body for between seven and twelve pounds.

In 1827, William Burke, an Irish labourer, was lodging at Log's boarding house in Tanner's Close in Edinburgh, and it was here that he became acquainted with William Hare, a tall, gaunt, sly-looking man. Burke was of shorter stature and more stoutly built. When a fellow lodger, an army pensioner, died still owing back rent the two men, with the their landlady Margaret Laird, hit on the idea of selling the lodger's body to Dr Knox, who lived at Surgeon's Square and had a reputation of paying well for bodies brought to him for dissection – with no questions asked. To the two men and Margaret this was a sensible and logical business deal. The lodger was dead and the money paid by Dr Knox would cover the back rent owed by the deceased. Burke and Hare opened the coffin, removed the body and replaced it with weighted sacks, then resealed the coffin ready for burial.

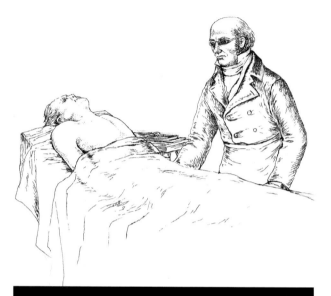

Dr Robert Knox (1791-1862) was disfigured by smallpox and blind in one eye. He had hundreds of students in Edinburgh and often had to repeat his lectures three times a day to accommodate them all. This meant he required a large number of body parts for dissection and demonstration. He was cleared of any suspicion of being involved in the murders.
R Dianne Sutherland

Not long afterwards another unfortunate lodger at Tanner's Close became ill. It appeared obvious to Burke and Hare that the lodger would eventually die. They were now impatient to earn another twelve pounds after their earlier success and decided to hasten the demise of the lodger by suffocation, leaving no obvious indication of murder. Another fresh body for Dr Knox, no questions asked, and cash in hand.

Their next victim was an elderly lady, Abigail Simpson, whom they befriended, took back to Tanner's Close and plied with alcohol. The following morning they poured more gin into the old lady until she was barely conscious and unable to resist suffocation. It is said that Dr Knox made no comment other than remarking on the fresh state of the corpse. Apparently, Burke and Hare made a profit of ten pounds, before deduction of the cost of gin. Heady with success, they next murdered a prostitute, Mary Haldane, using the same efficient method. On one occasion, they became a little too greedy and tried to double their profit on the same night. Two women who plied their trade on the streets were invited back to Tanner's Close. Mary Paterson cooperated by getting extremely drunk but her friend, Janet Brown, became suspicious and left. Mary Paterson, by now senseless with alcohol, was swiftly and efficiently dispatched and taken to Dr Knox. When Mary Paterson's body was lying on Dr Knox's dissecting table there was a tricky moment when one of his students claimed to recognise her from a previous night out. However, fast talking and quick work soon rendered the body unrecognisable.

With an increasing number of victims being swiftly processed Burke and Hare and their two female partners must have relished their new-found wealth. The killings continued for ten months, and although no one knows the final total it is thought to have been about sixteen. Living and working together in close proximity proved a strain on their relationship, however, and after a dispute Burke and Helen McDougal moved out of Tanner's Close to a house close to West Port. The friendship quickly returned to normal and it was soon 'business as usual'. However, success sometimes breeds carelessness.

One of the last to die was 'Daft Jamie', a pleasant man and well known on the city streets. His body was also recognised when laid out on Dr Knox's table. The curtain finally came down on their activities when Burke brought home Mrs Docherty. There were other people in the house at the same time enjoying a drinking session, and when the booze ran out the drinkers went off to buy more alcohol. While the house was empty, Burke and Hare seized the opportunity to murder Mrs Docherty. When the revellers returned they naturally enquired about the lady who had been there before, only to be told by Burke that she had decided to leave. However, it was noticed that Burke was a little edgy and insistent that no one should sit on the bed. In this party mood, and given Burke's attitude, sooner or later someone just had to look under the bed and find the body of Mrs Docherty. Burke, Hare, Laird and McDougal were arrested and committed for trial.

Hare and Laird saved their lives by turning King's Evidence, appearing as witnesses for the prosecution in Burke and McDougal's trial, which took place in December 1828. The trial lasted 24 hours, with the jury retiring to consider their verdict at 8.30am on Christmas Day. After 50 minutes' deliberation the jury found Burke guilty, and the charge against McDougal not proven. It is said that while awaiting execution Burke

William Hare as he appeared in court
Scottish National Portrait Gallery

HELEN M^c DOUGAL,
The
ASSOCIATE OF BURKE.

WILLIAM BURKE,
The
MURDERER.

William Burke and Helen McDougal, his common-law wife
Edinburgh City Libraries (NC)

asked if Knox would pay him an outstanding debt of five pounds due for the body of Mrs Docherty, so that he could purchase new clothes for his appearance on the scaffold. He was hanged at 8.15am on 28 January 1829 in torrential rain, in front of a crowd of nearly 30,000 at Liberton's Wynd, still complaining that Knox owed him five pounds. The *Times* of 2 February 1829 reported that Burke went to the gallows to 'vehement cheering from every quarter, mingled with groans and hisses'. His body was flayed and dissected, somewhat ironically, in the Edinburgh Medical College. Burke's skeleton hangs in the museum at Surgeons' Hall, Edinburgh, and also on display is a gold embossed pocketbook, covered with Burke's skin.

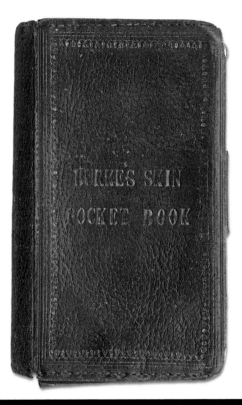

A pocketbook reputedly made from William Burke's skin from the
Surgeons' Hall, Edinburgh – Surgeons' Hall Museum

McDougal was freed after the 'not proven' verdict. Hare, as you might expect, was forced to flee Edinburgh and is believed to have ended up as a pauper on the streets of London. Robert Knox eventually found work as an anatomist at the Brompton Hospital and he died in 1862. Margaret Laird is thought to have returned to Ireland while Helen McDougal moved south to Newcastle and then County Durham, but her past always caught up with her and what happened to her is unknown. In the Scottish National Portrait Gallery in Edinburgh there is a display of phrenological heads in the library and the casts of heads includes those of Burke and Hare as well as the 'Ratho Murderer', George Bryce.

The defence counsel who acted for William Burke at his trial was David Milne Home (1805-1890) who went on to become Advocate–Depute from 1841-1845. His portrait by Charles Augustus Henry Lutyens (1829-1915), painted in 1870, hangs in the ante-room at Paxton House in the Scottish Borders.

Murder in Dundee

IN THE MID-NINETEENTH CENTURY DUNDEE WAS GROWING AT A RAPID PACE BECAUSE OF EXPANDING MANUFACTURING AND A DEVELOPING PORT. THE POPULATION WAS GROWING AND WEALTH WAS INCREASING; BUT SO WAS CRIME, REACHING ALMOST EPIDEMIC PROPORTIONS IN THE PERIOD BETWEEN 1820 AND 1840.

The Town Council appointed Town Officers who were responsible for patrolling the streets, keeping order and apprehending those who were 'up to no good'. It is against this background that watchman Duncan MacNab was on patrol during the night of Saturday 4 and the early hours of Sunday 5 August 1838.

Around one o'clock on the Sunday morning MacNab's route brought him to Thorter Row, a court containing several residential properties and the entrances of three public houses. Apart from several raised voices the area appeared deserted. MacNab continued on his patrol, returning later at about 1.30am, when he noticed what he at first thought was a drunk lying on the ground, but on closer examination he discovered it was the dead body of John Drew Woods, slumped at the bottom of a short flight of six steps leading up to the home of Arthur Woods, aged 60 and his younger wife Henrietta, stepmother to 21-year-old John.

The post-mortem showed that the deceased had suffered a fractured skull which would have rendered him unconscious, and he also had ligature marks around his neck. The conclusion was that he had been strangled after the blow to his head had occurred. The body was identified by police sergeant James Low, a friend of the deceased. The police were convinced that the solution was to be found in the immediate area. When Sergeant Low called on Arthur Woods to enquire about his son, he was surprised to find him fully dressed and wearing a hat, despite the early hour. When asked if he knew the whereabouts of his son he replied that he wasn't at home. However, his wife Henrietta said that John Drew had returned earlier but they had refused to open the door, adding that she did not know what had become of him but she thought she had heard him fall down the steps. At this point Mr Woods became defensive, emphasising that he had nothing to do with anything which may have happened to his son. The door of Wrights' Tavern opened onto the court and the landlady said she had heard a vicious argument in the Woods' home the previous week. She had gone over to find father and son locked in a furious fight while Henrietta was attempting to hit John Drew with a poker.

However, the most incriminating statement came from Mrs Scott, a resident of Thorter Row. She described how she had watched John Drew drunk, staggering towards his father's house, and then heard raised voices. John Drew was screaming, 'Don't choke me, father!' and she heard Arthur reply, 'I'll be your butcher before I sleep.' Then all went quiet. At this point she noticed the patrol man pass through the court. A subsequent search of the Woods' home uncovered several lengths of rope hanging from a hook on the pantry door. The pattern of one of these ropes was found to match exactly the marks on the neck of the dead man. Arthur and Henrietta Woods were charged with murder at the High Court in Edinburgh.

The trial of the couple was delayed until 25 February 1839 because Henrietta gave birth to a baby in the previous December. After all the evidence had been heard, the jury swiftly returned a verdict of guilty in respect of Arthur, after only thirty minutes' deliberation, and a 'not proven' verdict in Henrietta's case.

Arthur Woods was executed on Monday 25 March 1834. It appears that he addressed a short speech to a large crowd in which he maintained his innocence. As the hangman was removing the condemned man's neckerchief he asked him to send it to Henrietta as a keepsake.

Expenses relating to the execution of Arthur Woods included the erection of the scaffold at £40 7s 11d; payment of £17 5s to John Scott, the executioner; 14s 9d for meat for Scott while in attendance in the gaol; and £2 10s for his transport back to Edinburgh.

The High Court of Judiciary, Edinburgh – The Author

Behind bars at the High Court in Edinburgh – The Author

The Candle End Murder, Stirling

WHEN ALLAN MAIR FINALLY SNAPPED AND TURNED KILLER, HE WAS AN OLD MAN OF 84 YEARS. TODAY HE WOULD BE CLASSED AS A GERIATRIC CRIMINAL. WHEN HE WAS EXECUTED FOR HIS CRIME OF MURDER ON WEDNESDAY 4 MAY 1843 HE WAS, ALMOST CERTAINLY, ONE OF THE OLDEST MEN TO BE HANGED IN THE BRITISH ISLES IN THE NINETEENTH CENTURY. NOT ONLY WAS THE ATTENTION OF THE PUBLIC HELD BY REPORTS OF HIS AGE BUT ALSO BY THE GRIM ACCOUNTS OF MAIR, WHO WAS CRIPPLED WITH ARTHRITIS AND UNABLE TO WALK, BEING CARRIED TO THE GALLOWS IN A CHAIR.

Mair dispensed physical abuse to his wife Mary during the entire thirty years of their marriage, finally beating the last vestiges of life out of her with a stick in May 1843 at the house where they lived in Candle End,

Muiravonside, Stirling. An examination of the body in the morgue revealed she had been severely thrashed on her back, arms and legs, with repeated blows also to the head. When he was interrogated Mair denied all responsibility for the horrific beating of his wife. During his trial at Stirling Circuit Court a neighbour testified on oath to hearing Mair beating his wife: 'I could hear Mary shouting that she couldn't take any more.'

On being carried to the scaffold Mair harangued the executioner and officials in attendance, shouting, 'They've all told lies agin me, I'm nae murderer.' As Mair continued his rant, the executioner, John Murdoch, placed the rope around his neck. However, as he fell through the trapdoor the cord tying his hands together became undone, enabling him to grab the rope and delaying his death. Murdoch wrestled with Mair in a ghastly death struggle, eventually removing his hands from the rope. Mair took another minute or so to die. However, the story does not finish here.

During excavations in May 2000, a skeleton was discovered buried in the entrance to the prison courtyard. Forensic examination identified the remains as being those of Allan Mair and they were subsequently reburied in an unmarked grave.

The Dudsday Murder

IT WAS DUDSDAY IN KILMARNOCK, A COUNTRY FAIR WHEN LABOURERS AND SERVANTS WERE HIRED AND, ACCORDING TO THE *AYR ADVERTISER*, WHERE 'COUNTRY SERVANTS SPEND THEIR FORMER HALF YEAR'S WAGES ON NEW CLOTHES'. IT SHOULD HAVE BEEN A HAPPY TIME BUT FOR JAMES YOUNG AND HIS FAMILY THAT IS NOT HOW IT TURNED OUT.

James was born at Riccarton at a time when dates of birth were not always recorded, so it is thought that he was still a teenager when he met his death. His beaten body was found in Blackhill Road, near Gatehead in the parish of Dundonald in South Ayrshire, and not far from Forty Acres where he worked for farmer Joseph Smith. His assailant was eventually proved to be James McWheelan, who was also known as James McQueen. He was a gardener at Ardrossan for a time and then worked at the Glengarnock Iron Works.

It appears that James Young was attacked on Friday 26 or possibly Saturday 27 May 1848 near the Toll

Road leading from Forty Acres Toll Bar. It is here that the parish boundaries of Symington, Dundonald and Riccarton meet. The evidence indicates that Young was struck on the head several times with a stone or similar object, and then stabbed in the neck, which resulted in him bleeding to death. It was not a quick death as his hands were clutching lumps of earth and grass and he tried to claw his way to safety. Young's body was discovered lying in a pool of blood around four o'clock on Saturday morning by John Gebbie and John Scott. Gebbie and Scott reported their grisly discovery to the farmer at Forty Acres and the toll keeper, Robert Hendry, who were able to identify the body. Young's silver watch, chain and fifteen shillings in silver money were missing.

In some ways it is a bit strange that William Orr, a farmer, said he was riding past the Toll Bar between Beith and Paisley on the Sunday when he saw McWheelan hurriedly leaving the toll house. It later transpired that 35 pounds had been stolen and it was said that Young's watch had been pawned by an acquaintance of McWheelan. Apparently, William Orr was suspicious of McWheelan and had heard about the murder and the theft at Forty Acres Toll Bar, so he rode after McWheelan, apprehending him near Paisley and handing him over to the police.

Opposite page: Broadside concerning the proceedings of the Circuit Court of Judiciary, Ayr – National Library of Scotland

Ayr Autumn Circuit;

The Autumn Circuit was opened in the Court House, County Buildings, on Wednesday last October 4, 1848, by Lords Mackenzie and Medwyn.

WITH A FULL REPORT OF
THE TRIAL AND SENTENCE OF
M'WHEELAN
THE MURDERER !

—JAMES M'WHEELAN or M'Queen was placed at the bar on a charge of murder, as also robbery, in so far as, on the 26th or 27th of May last, when on or near the turnpike road, commonly called Black-hill Road, leading from Forty Acres Toll Bar, in one or more of the parishes of Dundonald, Riccarton, and Symington, in Ayrshire, he did wickedly and feloniously attack and assault James Young, then a farm servant in the employment of Joseph Smith, farmer, Forty Acres, and did, with a stone or some other instrument, strike the said James Young severe blows on or near the head, and did, with chisel or some other instrument, inflict a severe wound on or near his neck, to the great effusion of his blood, in consequence of which he immediately thereafter died, and was murdered by the said James M'Wheelan or M'Queen. He was farther charged with having, time and place above libelled, wickedly and feloniously, and by force and violence, taken from his pocket a silver watch, a steel or other metal chain, a watch key, a metal watch guard, and fifteen shillings in silver money.

There were no fewer than 93 witnesses cited for this case, which, from the peculiar barbarity and wantonness of the crime, excited a great interest. It commenced about twelve o'clock.

On being asked the question of guilty or not guilty the prisoner, an Irishman, and a rather good looking stoutly built man, said, in a firm voice, "not guilty." A jury was then empanelled, and the case went to trial.

A number of witnesses were then examined, whose evidence went to prove the charge.

THURSDAY, 5TH OCTOBER.

The Court met at nine o'clock this morning.

Mr. MAITLAND, counsel for the Crown, addressed to the jury. He commented with much emphasis upon the striking nature of the circumstantial evidence afforded in this case: in particular as to the chisel found near the scene of the murder—also, as to the position of the watch of the murdered man—and the napkin found on the road, all traced directly to the possession of the prisoner at one time or other not distant from the moment of the murder. He said that under a certain aspect circumstantial evidence was less liable to misconstruction than even direct testimony. He then went over the evidence in a very minute manner. He laid great stress upon the evidence of Thom, remarking that the time at which the prisoner met him was just sufficient to have allowed of his walking from the scene of the murder to the place wh re he overtook Thom. He commented on the general falsehood of the prisoners declaration. Harvey's evidence also he laid much stress upon, by which the prisoner's direct possession of the watch was not only corroborated but fully borne out in every particular by additional direct evidence. He spoke to the general intelligence and sagacity of the witnesses Scott and Gebbie, particularly alluding to their evidence in regard to the napkin found on the road, which, by a clear chain of evidence was proved to have been in prisoner's possession for a considerable time and on the morning previous to the murder. He then alluded to the exculpatory evidence, but contended that it was not at all conclusive.

Mr. BOYLE, in behalf of the prisoner, would admit that the watch had belonged to deceased and had been pledged at the instance of the prisoner, still it was not proved that he might not have got it from the true robber and murderer; he maintained there were no suspicious circumstances attending the pawning of the watch which had been pawned in the prisoner's own name. The chisel found proved nothing more thon that it was the instrument by which the murder was committed—nor had it been traced to the prisoner. The handkerchief was found at least a mile from the place of murder; it had no blood on it, and might not have been in any way connected with the murder. He contended that the exculpatory evidence of Wilson was of material importance, and commented at length upon the probability of the prisoner having lost his handkerchief, if it was really his, in passing the spot, before the murder was committed. As maintained that it was inconceivable that the murderer, reeking from the deed, covered with blood could be seen in Kilmarnock,—this was only spoken to by one witness, which by our law cannot prove any fact. The attempt to corroborate it had failed. He insisted upon the value and conclusiveness of the evidence furnished by the exculpatory witness, in relation to the prisoner's having blood of calves on his clothes, and that he had endeavoured to clean that off; he combatted the effort of the prosecutor to prove that the shaving off his whiskers was an attempt on his part to evade the officers of justice; he was never seen in company with James Young by any one, nor within three miles of the place where the murder occurred. Circumstantial evidence had been so usually defective that no work of fact or fiction had ever been written in which it was alluded to, where its inefficiency had not been demonstrated.

Lord MACKENZIE then addressed the jury at great length, carefully going over the evidence on both sides.

The Jury then retired, and after an absence of about half an hour returned into Court, and gave in a verdict unanimously finding the prisoner guilty as libelled.

Lord MACKENZIE then said—James M'Wheelan or M'Queen, it is now my painful duty to announce, that you have been convicted, by an unanimous verdict of the jury, of the whole crimes charged against you—that crime, being no less than murder and robbery. Robbery although a capital offence by the laws of Scotland, can be dealt with a milder; but the crime of murder can receive no mercy whatever. The punishment is capital. "He that sheddeth man's blood, by man shall his blood be shed." The law in this case, leaves me no dis retion, I must do my duty. You must, therefore, consider your life in this world at an end. A short time, and you will be conveyed to the scaffold. I can no d out no copes of pardon. Murder is always an atrocious crime. There remains for you no hope in t' is world. I cannot say t'at there will be no hope in the world which is to come. You must stand before the judgment seat of Almighty God, when you will have to answer for this crime. His Lordship then, in the usual form sentenced then prisoner, James M'Wheelan, or M'Queen, to be executed at Ayr, between the hoers of eight or ten o'clock, on the forenoon of the 26th October current.

At his trial in Ayr, McWheelan, who was described in a broadside – a sheet circulated by a printer – as being 'a good looking and stoutly built man', pleaded not guilty to all charges and 93 witnesses were called. The jury took only thirty minutes to find him guilty of murder and he was sentenced to death. After fifteen minutes of standing under the gallows with the rope around his neck and his head covered with a hood, McWheelan continued to pray. The hangman was uncertain when to pull the lever because James McWheelan was supposed to drop a handkerchief, in the usual fashion, to indicate he was ready. In exasperation, the Provost of Ayr shouted, 'Do your duty, executioner', and John Murdoch, the hangman, duly pulled the lever. McWheelan never admitted guilt and insisted upon his innocence to the last.

The Last Public Execution on Glasgow Green

IT WOULD APPEAR THAT DR EDWARD PRITCHARD'S AMBITION WAS TO BE THE MOST TALKED ABOUT MAN IN GLASGOW. HE WOULD EVENTUALLY ACHIEVE HIS AMBITION THROUGH NOTORIETY AFTER HAVING BEEN CONVICTED, IN JULY 1865, OF A DOUBLE MURDER.

Doctor Pritchard was a distinguished figure in Glasgow, not just as a doctor but as a writer and speaker who was not beyond stimulating his own popularity in curious ways. He admired the Italian revolutionary Garibaldi, who he claimed was a friend, and to support this he had a walking stick inscribed: 'To William Pritchard, from his friend General Garibaldi'. Pritchard, apparently, rarely missed an opportunity to show off this supposed gift.

On 5 May 1863 a fire broke out in the room of a servant girl, Elizabeth McGrain, aged 25, in Pritchard's house at 11 Berkeley Terrace, Glasgow. She allegedly died as a result of the fire, but as there appeared to have been no attempt to escape, there was a suspicion that she was unconscious or already dead before the fire started. Although the procurator fiscal examined the case no charges were levied and the doctor pocketed the insurance money.

When Dr Pritchard's wife Mary Jane Taylor, aged 38 and the daughter of a wealthy silk merchant, became ill in December 1864, he diagnosed gastric fever in consultation with Dr James Paterson. After showing no sign of recovery, Mary's 71-year-old mother, Jane Taylor, travelled from Edinburgh to help with the care of her daughter and her five children at 131 Sauchiehall Street, Glasgow. Jane Taylor became mysteriously ill while visiting the Pritchards and died on 28 February 1865. Mary Pritchard died a few weeks later on 18 March. It transpires that Dr Paterson was highly suspicious of the two deaths and refused to sign the death certificates, but he made no attempt to contact the relevant authorities to convey his suspicions. However, as a result of an anonymous letter, thought to have been written by Paterson, Pritchard was detained and arrested at Queen Street Police Station on 20 March. An exhumation of the two bodies revealed that the victims had been murdered using a lethal cocktail of tartarised antimony, aconite and opium.

Pritchard was tried at Edinburgh High Court with the trial commencing at 8am on 3 July 1865 and presided over by Lord Inglis. Public interest was intense, with special tickets being issued for the public gallery and additional space made available for reporters. *The Scotsman* newspaper reported Pritchard's appearance in court as 'sad and thoughtful' and 'cool and collected'. During the trial it was alleged that the doctor's wife had caught a servant, Mary MacLeod, and her husband together the previous November. It was shortly after this occasion that Mrs Pritchard became ill.

During the trial the prosecution proved that Pritchard had added antimony and aconite to an opium based preparation called Battley's Solution which was frequently used by Jane Taylor. Pritchard was found guilty of murder on both charges and sentenced to death. He was transported to Glasgow's North Prison where, *The Scotsman* reported, he admitted his guilt.

At 8am on the morning of 28 July 1865, Edward William Pritchard was the last man to be executed in public in Glasgow. Thousands of spectators gathered at the Saltmarket end of Glasgow Green to witness Pritchard's last moments. In normal circumstances a curtain was drawn around the space below the trap to enable the prisoner to die in privacy but on this occasion, in acknowledgement of the horrific nature of the crimes, the public were allowed to witness his final moments.

Nelson's Column in Glasgow Green. This column was built in 1806 by public subscription. From 1817 executions took place in front of the jail with the prisoner facing Nelson's Column and large crowds gathered in Glasgow Green to watch. – iStock

The executioner was William Calcraft, who was famed for his 'short drops' which resulted in the condemned being slowly strangled, taking up to five minutes to expire.

The executioner positioned the noose around Pritchard's neck, placed a white cap on his head and released the trap, dropping Pritchard to his death while women screamed and men cheered. The hangman climbed below and pulled on Pritchard's legs to ensure complete strangulation and, finally, Calcraft let go to cheering from the crowds as Pritchard's body spun round in slow motion.

The 'long drop' technique which broke the prisoner's neck was perfected by William Marwood in April 1872. Prior to this date execution by hanging was, in reality, strangulation on the end of a rope. In the case of Ruth Ellis, the last woman to be hanged in England at 9am on 13 July 1955, the executioner, Albert Pierrepoint, correctly calculated the 'drop' at 8 feet 4 inches (2.54 meters) with the whole process taking only twelve seconds.

In newspapers and other reports, Dr Pritchard was described as having a small round head. Phrenology – the theory that the shape and size of the head affected a person's character – was at its height at the time, and phrenologists suggested that he had a large amount of brain behind his ears and that this was an indication of a person who had criminal tendencies.

'A Lament for Dr Pritchard's Children' was published in a broadside in 1865 (first and last verses):

'Oh you kind hearted people think of Pritchard's children,
Who are five in number that are left to mourn,
For the loss of their mother that reared them so tender,
And their grandmother too who will never return.
For now in their grave they are consigned to slumber,
And soon hapless orphans forever they'll be,
For their father Dr Pritchard is sentenced for murder,
On the twenty-eight of July he must die on a tree.

Now the dice box of fate it has turned against Pritchard,
His time is short and his moments do fly,
For to pardon his sins for the crimes he committed,
On the Saviour of man all his hopes now doth lie.
Oh think of his orphans you kind hearted people,
And I hope there is none so heartless will be,
As to point with the finger of scorn towards them,
And say that their father, he died on a tree.'

The Ratho Murderer

JEANIE SEATON, AGED 23, WORKED AS A NURSEMAID AT A LARGE HOUSE OWNED BY MR AND MRS TOD, WHO ALSO EMPLOYED ISABELLA BROWN AS A COOK. THE HOUSE WAS SITUATED IN RATHO, A VILLAGE THROUGH WHICH THE UNION CANAL PASSES, IN A RURAL AREA, WEST OF EDINBURGH.

Jeanie and Isabella first met George Bryce, who worked as a carter in his father's coal business, at a dance in 1862. He was attracted to Isabella and they became friends. Bryce would see her when he delivered coal to the Tods' house as well as on social occasions. It appears that Isabella viewed the relationship as one of a casual nature, not least because, when they met, Jeanie was with her. On 10 March 1864 the three friends went on an outing to Edinburgh and at some point during the day Bryce began drinking excessively. This upset Isabella and she decided to break off their relationship. It would seem that soon after the Edinburgh day out, Bryce proposed marriage to Isabella. When she refused, he blamed Jeanie for exercising influence over her and warning her off him due to his excessive drinking. This feeling was reinforced over the following few weeks as each time he called on Isabella she was distinctly cool and withdrawn; all of which Bryce attributed to the influence of Jeanie.

On the night of 16 April Isabella was asleep in her room when she awoke startled to find that a windowpane had been broken. When she saw Bryce the next day she asked him if he had been responsible for breaking the glass, to which he is said to have replied, 'No, I knocked

The Bridge Inn, built in 1822, was a staging post on the Union Canal. The inn was owned by the father of the 'Ratho Murderer', George Bryce.
Royal Commission on the Ancient and Historical Monuments of Scotland

my head through it.' A week later, Bryce appeared to completely lose control, arriving at the Tods' house at 7pm, demanding to know the whereabouts of Jeanie. On discovering she was in the nursery he stormed in, threw Jeanie onto the floor and grabbed her by the throat. Meanwhile, Isabella's screams alerted Mrs Tod, who rushed into the nursery to witness Bryce hitting Jeanie on the head. Mrs Tod hastily grabbed an umbrella from a stand in the hallway and by repeatedly striking Bryce, managed to loosen his hold on Jeanie who immediately ran from the house, out of the back door. She took refuge on a neighbouring farm occupied by tenant farmer, Mrs Binnie.

Bryce, however, eventually cornered Jeanie, leaving her no room for escape. In her testimony, Mrs Binnie said she heard Jeanie screaming in terror. When Mrs Binnie arrived at the scene, she was greeted by a horrific scene. Bryce had his knee on Jeanie's shoulder while holding her by the neck, a razor in his hand and blood running from her throat. She died approximately ten minutes later. Bryce ran from the scene only to be apprehended later by Constable Peter Milne, about a mile west of Ratho.

Bryce was tried at Edinburgh on 31 May 1864 and found guilty of the murder of Jeanie Seaton, aged 23. Apparently the jury recommended mercy on the grounds of 'the low organisation of his mental faculties'. Nevertheless, he

Site of the Last Public Execution in Edinburgh

The site of the gallows is marked by the three brass plates set at the edge of the pavement in front of this notice. George Bryce, the Ratho Murderer, was executed here on 21st June 1864, the last public execution in Edinburgh.

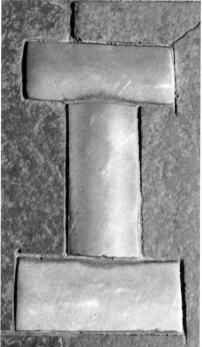

Above: Plaque on the wall on the corner of the High Street and George IV Bridge – The Author

Left: Three brass plates showing the site of the gallows – The Author

received a death sentence and on Tuesday 21 June at 8.40am Bryce was transported from High Street Gaol to Liberton's Wynd where, with St Giles Cathedral in the background, a scaffold had been erected. Public hangings were considered a popular entertainment and as large crowds gathered to see the spectacle, nearby taverns opened early in anticipation of extra business, which prompted a local newspaper to report that 'Many were the stray customers that were tempted hurriedly to avail themselves on the stale commodities of these establishments.'

At a few minutes before 9am, Bryce was escorted up the steps of the gallows where the hangman, Thomas Askern, placed a hood over Bryce's head, then the noose, and finally dropped him through the trapdoor. To the horror of the crowd Askern had miscalculated the drop, and the spectators watched the appalling sight of the victim swinging and struggling for almost four minutes, before finally choking to death. Because of Askern's bungled job, the police were obliged to provide him with a disguise and smuggle him out of Edinburgh.

At the junction of High Street and George IV Bridge in Edinburgh you will find a plaque on the wall and three brass plates set into the pavement marking the spot where Bryce was executed. He was the last criminal to be publicly hanged in Edinburgh.

An execution in Liberton's Wynd, Edinburgh around 1830
Edinburgh City Libraries

Broughty Ferry Murder Remains Unsolved

AFTER A REPORT FROM THE POSTMAN ABOUT AN OVERFLOWING LETTERBOX ON 3 NOVEMBER 1912, POLICE FORCED AN ENTRY INTO THE HOME OF MISS JEAN MILNE, A 65-YEAR-OLD EDWARDIAN LADY. THEY FOUND HER BODY, FULLY CLOTHED, LYING IN A POOL OF BLOOD AT THE FOOT OF THE STAIRS IN THE HALL OF HER MANSION, ELMGROVE HOUSE IN BROUGHTY FERRY.

There were all the indications of a violent death, a trail of bloodstains on the stairs and banisters, and blood splashed on the walls and floor. Jean Milne's head had signs of bruising and there was dried blood on her face. Although the injuries sustained were considered fairly slight, they were in aggregate enough to cause her death by causing a cerebral haemorrhage. Not only had her ankles been tied together with a curtain cord but her body had been partially covered by a sheet and a curtain had been fastened behind the glass door to prevent anyone from looking in. The telephone wire had been severed with garden shears which were discovered nearby, adding confusion to the sequence of events. Because of the complexity and spectacular nature of the crime, Detective Lieutenant John Trench of the Glasgow City Police was brought in to take charge of the investigation.

Although the autopsy suggested that Milne had been dead for about three weeks, it seems possible she had been alive for a time after the attack. Further details of this intriguing crime include the facts that there were no signs of theft and everything in the house was left undisturbed. Jean Milne was wearing jewellery, including rings, and the table had been laid for two people. The plates and cutlery were untouched and a meat pie on the table was intact. A half-smoked cigar was found in the dining room fireplace, possibly indicating the presence of male company, a theory supported by a local wine merchant who said that Milne had ordered wine and whisky, commenting that she was expecting a gentleman friend.

This gripping murder case is made up of a series of unanswered questions, and here is one more. The observant Detective Trench spotted something peculiar, in fact a real puzzler. When he was examining the clothes worn by Milne at the time of her death he noticed that there were numerous small holes, which he thought were consistent with a two-pronged carving fork, used with some force, an item which had been found partly hidden under a chest in the hall. As the autopsy report made no reference to any marks resembling stabbings, Trench requested an exhumation of the body. This request was refused and the question of the perforated clothing remains unresolved.

Jean Milne was a wealthy, fashionable lady, easy-going and considered slightly eccentric, who spent lengthy periods of leisure time in London, enjoying male company. The police discovered that Miss Milne had become acquainted with a man around forty years old, thought to be of German nationality, during a recent four-month visit to London. Shortly after returning home she had departed on a tour of the Scottish Highlands. A witness claimed to have seen her, on her return journey, on board the ship in the company of a tall man. Several witnesses claimed she had maintained her association with the mysterious tall man. A taxi driver recalled picking up a man in Dundee with an English accent on 15 October and dropping him off close to Elmgrove House. On the 16th, the following day, a refuse collector noticed a thin man about thirty years old leaving the house. There was also evidence that Miss Milne had met a 'stylish American' during her recent time in London.

When the Glasgow police contacted Scotland Yard for help in locating the American, events took a perplexing turn. Coincidentally a Canadian, Charles Warner, was in custody in Kent for non-payment of restaurant bills. When a photograph of Warner was shown to the witnesses in Broughty Ferry, they confirmed he was the man, despite their previous vague descriptions. Meanwhile, in London there was an eyewitness parade of people who had seen Jean and her companion in The Strand Palace Hotel and The Bonnington Hotel. Interestingly, nobody recognised Warner. Detective Trench travelled to Kent and arrested Warner on his release. On the return journey to Dundee, Trench had plenty of time to talk to Warner, who continued to vigorously protest his innocence, leaving Trench unconvinced of his guilt.

Warner claimed he had arrived in London on 18 October having previously been in Antwerp. Unfortunately he was unable to provide proof because he had been travelling alone and sleeping rough and therefore did not possess any hotel bills. However, he did remember that he had pawned a waistcoat in Antwerp on 16 October and, crucially, he still had the ticket. The dedicated Trench travelled to Antwerp to check the ticket against the pawnshop records, redeem the waistcoat and bring it back to Dundee. Warner was subsequently released without charge and returned to Canada on 13 January. This murder case remains unsolved.

Army Deserters Hanged for Murder

DURING THE 1920S, GLASGOW HIGH COURT WAS THE STAGE FOR A NUMBER OF SENSATIONAL MURDER TRIALS. ONE WHICH FASCINATED THE PUBLIC AND INCREASED NEWSPAPER SALES WAS THE TRIAL OF TWO MEN CALLED ALBERT JAMES FRASER AND JAMES ROLLINS.

Fraser was aged 24, a deserter from the Australian Army, and described as tall with a sallow complexion and heavy eyebrows. Rollins was an Irishman, aged 22, of shorter stature than Fraser, clean shaven, and a deserter from the British Army. They were charged with robbing and murdering Henry Senior on Tuesday 3 February 1920. Henry was 35 years old, unmarried and a war veteran with honourable service. Fraser and Rollins both pleaded not guilty.

Fraser and Rollins were working one of the oldest criminal ploys. They employed two girls, and one or the other would pick up a stranger in a bar and entice him out to a shadowy back lane or darkened area in a park. On Thursday morning, 5 February, two boys playing football in Queen's Park Recreation Ground discovered the body of Henry Senior behind a clump of bushes. The killers had taken his cash, overcoat, shoes, hat and a yellow pig-skin notebook. The post-mortem report, carried out by Professor John Glaister, stated that the victim had suffered extensive external and internal injuries including extensive liver damage, consistent with being violently kicked while on the ground.

Queen's Park, Glasgow – St Andrews University

Police enquiries revealed that two men, late on the evening of Tuesday 3 February, had been seen boarding a tram near the recreation ground. The tram conductor particularly recalled seeing the two men because one of them had a shoe in each coat pocket. Senior's shoes were eventually traced to a pawnshop and the owner was able to provide a detailed description of the men who had brought them in. Routine detective work paid dividends when two men matching the descriptions, accompanied by two women, were spotted in Glasgow Central Station boarding the Belfast boat-train. News of this sighting reached Police HQ on Saturday afternoon, 7 February. Detective Superintendent Andrew Keith, with little time to spare, managed to board the next boat-train, arriving in Belfast early Sunday morning on the trail of four suspects with only vague descriptions for identification. Fortunately, on arrival the Belfast police were able to report sightings of the suspects living rough in the city's Cave Hill Park. Fraser and Rollins had decided to live rough to avoid capture but their plan did not work. The two women were later apprehended in the comfort of a city centre hotel.

The trial at Glasgow High Court commenced on Tuesday 4 May 1920. The court was reportedly packed with spectators, with hundreds more unable to gain admission. Fraser and Rollins were charged with murder and the two women, Helen White, aged 23, and Elizabeth Stewart, 19, as accomplices. Crucially for the

Glasgow High Court
of Judiciary – iStock

prosecution, White and Stewart turned King's Evidence and were included in the 52 witnesses called on behalf of the Crown. In the course of her evidence, White stated that on the night of Tuesday 7 February the accused had told her to get a man and they would then follow her to Queen's Park Recreation Ground.

White described how she saw Rollins approach Senior from behind, putting one arm round his neck and pulling him back while Fraser hit him with his fists and a revolver. She went on to state how she met the accused in Central Station and that Rollins was carrying a man's coat and shoes. When she was handed the coat she noticed it was bloodstained. She queried the bloodstains with Fraser and he allegedly replied that it belonged to the man they had 'done in' in the park. The following day Fraser and White washed the coat in an attempt to remove the stains and later she pawned the coat for seventeen shillings. White also said she thought Rollins had pawned Senior's shoes. In addition Elizabeth Stewart stated that while in Belfast, Rollins appeared upset and said, 'It is awful to be the cause of the death of a man.' After the medical evidence had been given by Professor Glaister, the case for the prosecution was concluded. There were no witnesses for the defence. However, Mr George Martin KC, who was defending the accused, claimed that three additional charges had been introduced simply to create the impression that the prisoners were known as robbers and thieves.

The jury retired at 2pm, returning after just 19 minutes and finding Fraser and Rollins guilty of murder. The judge, Lord Sands, donned the black cap and passed the death sentences. The murderers were simultaneously executed by hangman John Ellis on 26 May 1920. It was reported that the two men maintained a composed demeanour as the white hoods were placed over their heads. Apparently, Fraser's last words to Rollins were, 'Cheer up', just as the lever to open the trapdoors was about to be pulled.

Professor John Glaister (1856-1932), who carried out the postmortem in this case and appeared as an expert witness, was Professor of Forensic Medicine at the University of Glasgow from 1898 to 1931. In 1902, he wrote the 'Textbook of Medical Jurisprudence, Toxicology, and Public Health' which included the use of fingerprints in identifying criminals.

An Edinburgh Murder and a Life of Crime

JOHN DONALD MERRETT WAS BORN IN NEW ZEALAND IN 1908 BUT WHEN HIS PARENTS SEPARATED HE ACCOMPANIED HIS MOTHER, WHO RETURNED TO ENGLAND. 'DONNIE' ENROLLED IN MALVERN COLLEGE IN 1924 AND AT THE AGE OF SEVENTEEN HE WAS TALL, MATURE LOOKING – AND A WOMANISER.

On 10 March 1926 he moved with his mother Bertha to 31 Buckingham Terrace, Edinburgh. She was comfortably off with about £700 a year and at 21 Donnie would inherit a considerable sum of money from his grandfather. Bertha was sure her son was attending Edinburgh University, but in fact he spent his time at the Dunedin Palais de Danse in Picardy Place. Donnie was a regular customer, booking his favourite hostess at 30 shillings per night or 15 shillings per afternoon, prices that were way beyond his weekly allowance of 10 shillings from his mother.

Henrietta Sutherland, Bertha's maid, arrived for work on 17 March at the usual time of 9am and soon after heard a single gunshot. According to her testimony, she heard books falling followed by a distraught Donnie rushing into the kitchen and announcing that his mother had shot herself because she had just opened a letter from her bank which disclosed that he had been forging his mother's signature on cheques. Henrietta stated that Mrs Merrett was lying on the floor, alive but bleeding profusely from a head wound. The sharp-eyed Henrietta also said she noticed a pistol lying on the top of a bureau in the room. However, variations in Henrietta's evidence and inconsistencies in the police account begin to emerge. The reported sequence of events appears to be as follows.

Following a call to the police reporting the incident, two constables arrived at the flat. One of them picked up the weapon, a .25 Spanish automatic, wrapped it in newspaper and placed it in his pocket, but when interviewed later he could not recall whether he had found it on the floor or on the bureau. Merrett, however, said he had picked up the gun and placed it on the bureau before entering the kitchen. Perplexingly, that same afternoon, when questioned by Detective Inspector Fleming, Henrietta changed her story. She apparently said that on hearing the gunshot she had gone into the lobby in time to observe, through an open door, Mrs Merrett falling out of her chair to the floor and the gun slipping from her hand. The detective discovered two letters from Mrs Merrett's bank informing her of her overdrawn account. Mystifyingly, in a third statement made by Henrietta a few days later, she reverted to the facts given in her original version.

As suicide was unlawful at that time, Bertha was placed on a secure ward and when she complained of a pain in her ear she was told she had suffered an accident. In a period of lucidity, during which she had a conversation with a doctor, Bertha recalled that her son had been standing beside her when a loud explosion seemed to go off in her head. The doctor reported the conversation to Inspector Fleming, but he took no action. After Bertha's death on 1 April, a post-mortem performed by Professor Littlejohn reported that the position of the entry wound was unusual for suicide. The absence of blackening and tattooing led him to deduce that the gun was likely to have been fired by a third party.

Bertha's sister, Mrs Penn, and her husband stayed in the Edinburgh flat to look after Donnie, who continued his relationship with Betty Christie, a dance instructor at the Palais de Danse. When Donnie's welfare passed to the Public Trustee, they arranged for him to live at the vicarage of Hughenden, in Buckinghamshire. The Office of the Public Trustee was required to assess Mrs Merrett's assets and this was to be the undoing of Donnie. During the eight weeks before the shooting, he had cashed cheques to the value of £360. A warrant for his arrest was issued on 29 November 1926, and he was detained and returned to Edinburgh.

At his trial on 1 February 1927 he was charged with the murder of his mother and forging her signature on 29 cheques, totalling £457.3s.6d. Apparently, he had spent £139 of this money to purchase a motorcycle and sidecar while his mother was dying in hospital from the gunshot wound. Merrett's defence counsel, Craigie Atchison KC, put on a dazzling performance, shredding the prosecution's allegations and emphasising that during police investigations Henrietta Sutherland had testified that she had seen Mrs Merrett falling to the floor with the pistol still in her hand. Although the trial lasted seven days, it took the jury only 55 minutes to return a verdict of not proven on the murder charge. However, there was a unanimous verdict of guilty on the charge of forgery. Eighteen-year-old Donnie was sentenced to twelve months in prison. When released in October 1927, he was offered accommodation by Mrs Bonner, a friend of his late mother who had a spare room and a 17-year-old daughter, Vera. Within 18 months the pair had eloped and married in Glasgow; and a few months later both had been arrested for obtaining goods by false pretences.

On his 21st birthday Merrett inherited £50,000 from his grandfather's estate, just before serving six months in Durham prison for deceit. The money was quickly squandered and in the 1930s he was involved in smuggling drugs and arms between Malta, North Africa and Spain. At the beginning of the Second World War he joined the Royal Naval Volunteer Reserve, quickly becoming a commander of a motor gunboat. His responsibility included a schooner based in Alexandria running supplies into Tobruk under German gunfire, simultaneously making money for himself. His ship was sunk and he was taken prisoner, which meant that he avoided a court martial.

Merrett was now calling himself Ronald John Chesney and he purchased a war surplus, ex-German Navy E-boat for cross-Channel 'business' activities, ending up spending three months in Pentonville Prison for importing duty-free nylon stockings, followed by twelve months in Wandsworth Prison for similar activities.

In the 1950s, short of cash, he considered how he could get hold of £10,000 available in a 'survivor takes all' trust fund which he had set up with his wife, Vera. Merrett conceived a 'cunning plan' which he put into operation in February 1954. He travelled from Germany to Ealing, where there was a reconciliation with Vera involving a considerable quantity of alcohol, terminating with Vera drowning in her bath. His plan received a setback as, just before he left the house, his mother-in-law, 72-year-old Mary Menzies, arrived. Desperate to prevent her from discovering Vera's body, he struck her with a pewter tankard and strangled her. After concealing her body he quickly left and five days later returned to Cologne, confident he would escape detection. However, his confidence was misplaced. Vera's body and that of her mother were discovered the following day.

The police quickly established that Chesney and Merrett were the same person and a murder hunt was soon under way. On reading the news of a double murder hunt, Merrett must have thought that the game was up and may have come to the conclusion that the only outcome would be the hangman's noose. He wrote several last letters, including an affectionate farewell to Sonia, his latest girlfriend, who was the daughter of a Cologne greengrocer. On 16 February 1954, on the bank of the River Rhine, Merrett placed the muzzle of a Colt revolver in his mouth and squeezed the trigger. His body was unclaimed, but in a gruesome finale the Metropolitan Police asked for his badly scratched forearms so that they could establish that the flesh found under the fingernails of Mary Menzies was that of Merrett. Today, Donald Merrett's forearms are preserved in formaldehyde in a clear plastic container, standing on a shelf in the Black Museum at Scotland Yard.

The High Court of Judiciary, Edinburgh
The Author

Police Officer and Murderer

A TAXI DRIVER TRAVELLING ALONG PROSPECTHILL ROAD, GLASGOW IN THE EARLY HOURS OF A WET FRIDAY MORNING ON 28 JULY 1950 RECEIVED AN UNPLEASANT SHOCK WHEN HE STOPPED TO INVESTIGATE A LARGE BUNDLE IN THE CENTRE OF THE ROAD, ONLY TO FIND THAT IT WAS THE BODY OF A WOMAN. THE FIRST POLICE OFFICER WHO ARRIVED ON THE SCENE, PC WILLIAM KEVAN, INSTINCTIVELY THOUGHT IT WAS NOT A HIT AND RUN ACCIDENT.

His inclination was confirmed by the results of the post-mortem performed by Professor Andrew Allison, who established that the deceased female had suffered extensive injuries to her upper torso, including broken ribs and injuries to her face and skull. Crucially, there was no indication of injuries to her legs, which would have been expected if she had been hit while standing in the path of an oncoming vehicle. There was also no sign of injury to her hands, as would be expected if she attempted to break her fall after having been struck by a vehicle. Further examination of the body revealed injuries to her right temple, suggesting she had been knocked unconscious before being run over. The pattern of blood distribution, coupled with multiple tyre marks on the road, suggested that the victim had been repeatedly run over by a car. A simple hit and run would leave the victim with broken legs, which was not the case here, and only one set of tyre marks at either side of the body.

There was no identification on the body, which was unusual in post-war Britain where people were still in the habit of carrying some means of identification. After Glasgow Police released information to the newspapers appealing for help in identifying the body, Mrs Johnston, a friend of the victim, came forward and identified the body as that of her friend Catherine McCluskey, aged 40, a single parent with two older children, each by a different father. A casual remark made by Mrs Johnston as she was leaving the police station alerted the police. She said that Catherine had been planning to settle down with her new man, Mr Robertson, who was a policeman. It didn't take the investigating officers long to track down PC James Robertson, a married man who owned an Austin saloon car. A forensic examination of the underside of the vehicle revealed blood, tissue fragments and remnants of clothing. Robertson was charged with

Prison van entering Barlinnie – Newsquest (Herald & Times)

murder, which he denied, and although he admitted to knowing Catherine McCluskey, he denied having an affair with her or killing her.

At his trial on 6 November 1950 he claimed in his defence that he had sneaked off shift to see Catherine that night and had hidden his car up a street, close to his beat. Robertson went on to claim that when they met they had a furious argument, which resulted in him driving off at excessive speed in a temper. He claimed that he almost immediately felt bad about the squabble, braked hard and reversed back to where Catherine was standing, but travelled back too far and became aware of a bump. Getting out of the car, he realised he had run over Catherine and then drove off in a panic. He then rejoined his partner on the beat as if nothing had happened.

The prosecution evidence was strong and persuasive, with the defending lawyer facing a formidable task. The police evidence, apart from blood and clothing on the underside of the car, showed that the car was stolen and carried false number plates. A serving police officer shown to be a thief and a liar, coupled with forensic evidence suggesting he had severely beaten Catherine McCluskey with his truncheon, was enough to convince the jury of his guilt. The jury made no recommendation for mercy and his appeal against the conviction failed.

James Ronald Robertson, a serving police officer, walked his last thirteen steps from the condemned cell to the execution chamber in Barlinnie Prison, Glasgow, on 16 December 1950 to meet his fate at the hands of Albert Pierrepoint, the official hangman, who took pride in being quick and efficient.

HMP Barlinnie is known locally as the Bar-L or the Big Hoose. It was built over 130 years ago on what was the Barlinnie Farm Estate in Riddrie. At that time it was in the countryside and far from Glasgow's tenements. Between 1882 and 1897 four residential halls (houseblocks) along with an impressive chapel were built. It may seem strange but somehow the 'street' with the old stone buildings still has a rural village feel about it. Over the years many extensions and alterations have taken place. This is now a very busy establishment with 8,000 prisoner admissions every year as it receives prisoners from the courts in the west of Scotland.

A former Governor, Derek McGill, was quoted in 'The Scotsman' newspaper as saying, 'This is not just a prison. This is Barlinnie.'

He Murdered the Family and then Fed the Cat

PETER MANUEL WAS BORN IN 1927 IN NEW YORK TO SCOTTISH PARENTS WHO HAD GONE TO AMERICA DURING THE DEPRESSION TO FIND WORK. THEY RETURNED TO SCOTLAND WHEN HE WAS AROUND SIX YEARS OLD, BY 1937 THE FAMILY WERE LIVING IN COVENTRY.

Peter struggled at school and played truant. By the time he was 11 years old, he was on probation for breaking into a shop. At 15 he broke into a house and after stealing a purse, beat a sleeping girl with a hammer. He was sent to an approved school but ran away several times and on one of these occasions mugged and assaulted a woman. Afterwards he fled to Glasgow, where he was arrested and sent to borstal.

When he was released in 1945, he returned to his parents' home, which was now in Lanarkshire. The seriousness of his offences increased from housebreaking to attacking an expectant mother. From the age of 18, Manuel spent the next eight years in Peterhead Prison, where the inmates were sent to work in granite quarries.

In 1955 Manuel was back in court for assault and conducted his own defence. The jury returned a not proven verdict. Manuel frequently sought attention from the police and contacted them to say that he had met a spy while in Peterhead Prison who knew details about Burgess and Maclean, the spies who had defected. This information was passed to MI5 and the FBI, who interviewed Manuel but soon realised that there was no substance to his claims.

In January 1956, the body of 17-year-old Anne Kneilands was found on a golf course in East Kilbride with her skull smashed with an iron bar. Manuel was questioned but not charged. In September 1956, Marion Watt, her daughter Vivienne and her sister Margaret Brown were murdered in their beds, shot while sleeping in their home at Fennsbank Avenue, Glasgow. William Watt, husband and father, was arrested and remanded in Barlinnie Prison, where Manuel was serving a sentence for break-ins. Manuel played a cat-and-mouse game with Watts, discussing the murder, speaking with his solicitor and giving statements to the press. Watts was released but Manuel was not charged with these murders until January 1958.

In 1957, Sydney Dunn was found near the wreckage of his taxi in County Durham. He had been shot in the back of his head and had his throat cut. It was many months later that Manuel was picked out by witnesses in an identification parade, but this case never came to court.

In December 1957, Isabelle Cooke, a pupil at Hamilton Academy, disappeared and it was only when Manuel was arrested in January 1958 that he led the police to the place where he had strangled and buried her.

On New Year's Day 1958, Peter Smart, his wife Doris and their son Michael were shot as they slept in their beds in their home in Sheepburn Road, Uddingston, Glasgow. Manuel spent several days in their house after killing the Smarts, making himself meals, using the family car and even feeding their cat. When he was arrested for these murders Manuel confessed to murdering the Watts family, Anne Kneilands and Isabelle Cooke. The guns used were found by police divers in the River Clyde where Manuel told them to search.

When his trial began on 12 May 1958, Manuel appeared dressed in a black blazer, blue trousers, grey shirt and tie. Unexpectedly, Manuel pleaded not guilty to all charges, dismissed his counsel and conducted his own defence once again. The jury found Manuel guilty of seven murders but not the murder of Anne Kneilands.

Peter Manuel enters the High Court in Edinburgh through the
rear entrance – The Scotsman Publications Ltd

He never stood trial for the murder of Sydney Dunn although the English police were waiting to arrest him for this crime if he was released by the Scottish court.

It is said that while in Barlinnie Prison he confessed to two more killings in Glasgow and one in London. On 11 July 1958, at the age of 31 and after spending a large part of his life in penal institutions, Peter Manuel walked the few steps from the condemned cell to the execution chamber in Barlinnie Prison where the noose awaited him. His body was buried within the confines of the prison.

Manuel's chief executioner was Harry Allen (1911-1992) who always wore a bow tie during executions as a sign of respect. He was assistant executioner to Albert Pierrepoint until 1956 and he prided himself that his executions were swift and humane.

On the day that he executed Manuel his wife for over 20 years, Marjorie Clayton, left him.

Allen's most controversial case was that of James Hanratty convicted of the 'A6 murder' in 1962. However, in 2001, DNA evidence linked Hanratty to the crime scene.

The last hanging in Scotland was carried out by Allen at Craiginches Prison in Aberdeen.

Condemned Cell in Aberdeen 'Like the Ritz!'

THOMAS GUYAN, A MERCHANT SEAMAN, MARRIED MARGARET MAY ON 2 FEBRUARY 1957 AND IN 1958 THEY MOVED INTO A FIRST-FLOOR FLAT AT 14 JACKSON TERRACE, ABERDEEN, OWNED BY MARGARET'S GRANDMOTHER, ANNIE HENDERSON. MARGARET BECAME PREGNANT, BUT NOT BY HER HUSBAND, AND IN FEBRUARY 1961 GAVE BIRTH TO A SECOND CHILD. AFTER A NUMBER OF ARGUMENTS SHE SOUGHT LEGAL ADVICE ABOUT THE POSSIBILITY OF DIVORCE BUT THOMAS, HER HUSBAND, REFUSED TO CONSIDER THE PROSPECT.

As Margaret continued to struggle with her fragile marriage she took a job in December 1961 at John R. Stephen Fish Curers, where she met fair-haired Henry Burnett, who quickly became an admirer. Burnett was soon to find himself playing a central role in a complex love triangle with two other participants, 25-year-old Margaret and her husband Thomas, aged 27.

A relationship developed between the pair and in early April 1963 Margaret moved out of the flat in Jackson

Terrace, taking her younger son Keith, and moved to Skene Terrace with Burnett. This arrangement proved to be unsuccessful, possibly due to Burnett's jealous nature, possessiveness and unstable personality, which led to him locking Margaret in the house each time he went out. As a result of a chance encounter on 31 May with her estranged husband, Thomas, who had never wanted a separation, Margaret decided to return to him after he suggested a reconciliation. She went back to Skene Terrace at 4pm on the same day with her friend, 66-year-old Georgina Cattanagh, who came along for moral support. Margaret opened the door and she was shocked to find Burnett inside. When she explained that she was returning to her husband Burnett was furious and screamed: 'Margaret, Margaret, you are not going to leave me!' In a rage, fuelled by jealousy, he grabbed a knife and held it to Margaret's throat. Mrs Cattanagh, who was locked outside, thumped furiously on the door while shouting at Burnett to release Margaret. A few minutes later Burnett ran out, leaving Margaret shocked but unharmed. She then left, accompanied by Mrs Cattanagh, and headed for Jackson Terrace.

In the meantime, Burnett, intent on revenge, went to his brother's house in the Bridge of Don area as he knew Frank had a shotgun. Burnett broke open the gun cabinet and removed the weapon and ammunition. Apparently, he then boarded a number fourteen bus going towards Jackson Terrace. On arrival, he pushed his way into the flat as Mrs Cattanagh screamed: 'You can't come in here!' At this point Thomas Guyan opened the kitchen door to see what was happening and at that moment Burnett shot him in the head, killing him instantly.

Burnett then gripped Margaret's arm and ran with her from the flat, pulling her down a lane as far as a petrol station in Seaforth Road. A local resident was filling his vehicle with petrol when Burnett insisted he hand over his vehicle, reportedly saying, 'Is this your car, pal? I'll take it now.' As Burnett and Margaret quickly sped off, Burnett proposed marriage. At the trial Margaret said she had agreed to marry him. The police quickly located the vehicle and followed the pair north towards Peterhead. After travelling about fifteen miles Burnett pulled over near Ellon and, offering no resistance, was arrested.

Burnett's trial ran from 23 to 25 July 1963 and his barrister claimed a defence of insanity or alternatively diminished responsibility. In addition, his mother described his disturbed childhood and how as a boy he had played truant, threatened his sisters with a knife, and on one occasion tried to commit suicide. Extensive medical evidence included a statement from two doctors saying that, after his suicide attempt, Burnett had signed himself into a mental hospital and, in their opinion, he had been of unsound mind at the time of the murder. However, as Burnett had used a gun it was capital murder, and as he had stolen the gun this was considered clear evidence of premeditation. The jury retired and returned twenty-five minutes later with a verdict of guilty of murder.

The court heard testimony from three psychiatrists, who all agreed that Burnett should not receive the death sentence on psychiatric grounds. This opinion was further reinforced by letters sent to the press from two of the expert witnesses at the trial explaining further that the evidence suggested that Burnett displayed psychopathic tendencies. It would appear that the expert medical evidence was ridiculed by the press and discounted by the Crown. In the 1950s, the argument for capital punishment was pivotal upon the use of a firearm: murder by firearm was a capital offence. The intention was to deter criminals from armed robbery. The expert witnesses argued that Burnett's crime was an impulsive crime of passion and not the type of crime motivated by the intentions that capital punishment was intended to deter. After receiving the death sentence, the families of both Burnett and Guyan petitioned for his reprieve, but to no avail. On 14 August, the day before his execution, Henry Burnett and Margaret Guyan were allowed a thirty-minute meeting for a final farewell in Craiginches Prison. As this was the first hanging in Aberdeen since 1891, a new condemned suite had to be constructed. Burnett apparently told Margaret it was 'like the Ritz!'

At 8am on Thursday 15 August 1963, 21-year-old Henry John Burnett was executed on Britain's newest gallows in Craiginches Prison. The hangman was Harry Allen, assisted by Samuel Plant. Burnett was the 34th and last person to be hanged in Scotland in the twentieth century. Burnett's body was buried in an unmarked grave within the prison and when the establishment was closed in January 2014 his remains were exhumed and cremated at Aberdeen Crematorium.

The 'Orders for Executing the Death Sentence on 15 August 1963' included:

The executioners, Mr Allen and Mr Plant will be accommodated in the Chief Officers Room and not leave the prison until after the execution. Aberdeen County Council will supply them with a 'quantity of alcoholic refreshments'. Burnett will be provided with his own clothing the night before with the exception of his collar and tie. The Medical Officer can give permission for Burnett to be offered a 'stimulant' about 7.30am. Baillies Stephen and Middleton and the Deputy Chief Constable McQueen will meet in the Governor's Office and will be taken to the Execution Chamber at 7.57am. 'Should a stimulant be required Aberdeen County Council will provide.' On the afternoon of the 14 August a grave will be dug 'in the recess between the pit room and the staff room toilets'. On the morning of the execution the prison will be on lock down from 7.30am until 9.30am - all prisoners locked up and no cars permitted to park on the entrance drive. The prison officers who will escort Burnett to the execution chamber will be excused further duties that day.

Bible John

GLASGOW'S BARROWLAND BALLROOM WAS A POPULAR DANCEHALL AND JUST THE PLACE FOR A GOOD NIGHT OUT. HOWEVER, FOR THREE WOMEN WHO DANCED WITH JOHN, A MAN AROUND SIX FEET TALL, WITH REDDISH-AUBURN HAIR, BLUE-GREY EYES, AND WEARING A SMART SUIT, IT WAS TO LEAD TO THEIR DEATHS.

On at least one occasion John had a friend with him, who was known as 'John from Castlemilk', a large housing estate on the outskirts of the city. In October 1969 Helen Puttock and her sister Jean Langford were enjoying a night at the dancing when they met the two Johns in Barrowlands. Afterwards, the man from Castlemilk left them to catch a bus home and the three walked to Glasgow Cross to find a taxi. John appeared caring and charming and told the girls that he worked in a laboratory, didn't drink and his parents were very religious, so he knew all about the bible. The taxi dropped Jean off at her house in Knightswood and continued on with 'Bible' John and Helen to Scotstoun. Helen's body was found in a back court in Earl Street near where she lived. She had been strangled. There

The refurbished Barrowland Ballroom reopened in 1960 after being gutted by fire in 1954. It was as popular as ever, crowded and atmospheric.
Newsquest (Herald & Times)

was a bite mark on her leg and her handbag was missing. This was the third time this killer had struck.

Patricia Docker was not seen alive after she left the Barrowland in February 1968. What happened next is still unknown but her body was found in Carmichael Place, near her home in Langside Place. She had been strangled and her handbag was missing. The bag was found some time later dumped in the River Clyde.

In August 1969 the body of Jemima McDonald was found in MacKeith Street in a derelict building. She had been beaten and strangled and her handbag, purse and scarf were missing. Jemima had been dancing at Barrowland that evening and left around midnight with a man with reddish-auburn hair, dressed in a blue suit and white shirt.

Despite police investigations no one has ever been charged with these murders and there is speculation as to why this apparent serial killer stopped killing. Perhaps he was frightened off by the publicity and investigations, maybe he left Scotland or it might be that he was arrested and imprisoned for other offences. The murders remain unsolved.

Bibliography

Baggoley, M. (2013) *Scottish Murders*, Stroud: The History Press.

Buchanan, K. (2014) *Bradwell's Eclectica Glasgow*, Sheffield: Bradwell Books.

Dalhousie, F. (2014) *Bradwell's Eclectica Edinburgh*, Sheffield: Bradwell Books.

Hamilton, J. (2011) *Scottish Murders*, Glasgow: Waverley Books.

Knox, B. (1968) *Court of Murder*, London: John Long Ltd.

Wallis, L. and Wright, D. (2011) *Scottish Murders*, Broxburn: Lomond Books.

www.murderpedia.org

www.capitalpunishmentuk.org

Acknowledgements

Many thanks to researcher John Sanderson for delving into the murky world of murders in Scotland and to Sean McFedries for his knowledge of prisons and executions.

Thank you also to the helpful staff at the National Library of Scotland, the Scottish National Portrait Gallery, and the People's Story Museum in Edinburgh.

Last night there wis a murder in a fish shop

Last night there wis a murder in a fish shop,
A wee dug stole a haddie bone,
A big dug tried tae take if aff her,
So Ah hit it wi' a tattie scone.

(Traditional children's rhyme)

Other books in the Bradwell Books Murder Stories series

AVAILABLE NOW

Derbyshire Murder Stories

Leicestershire Murder Stories

Lincolnshire Murder Stories

Nottinghamshire Murder Stories

South Wales Murder Stories

Staffordshire Murder Stories

Yorkshire Murder Stories

BRADWELL
BOOKS

For more details of these books and other books you may be
interested in, visit www.bradwellbooks.com